better together*

*This book is best read together, grownup and kid.

 akidsco.com

a
kids
book
about

a kids book about

CONSENT

by Karli Johnson

**a
kids
book
about**

Printed in the United States of America.

A Kids Book About books are available online: *akidsco.com*

To share your stories, ask questions, or inquire about bulk
purchases (schools, libraries, and nonprofits), please use
the following email address: *hello@akidsco.com*

ISBN: 978-1-958825-07-5

Designed by Rick DeLucco
Edited by Emma Wolf

Interested in inviting Karli to speak at your school,
organization, or event? Visit www.karlijohnson.com.

For Ollie—never stop asking.

And for everyone who's ever had
their "no" ignored. I believe you.
And it's not your fault.

Intro

When most adults hear the phrase "consent education," they first assume "sex education." Of course, consent must always be asked for and granted for physical touch and intimacy, but consent education is so much more and needs to be taught (and mastered) well before high school sex ed.

Petting a cat, eating someone's food, borrowing a toy, entering someone's room. We have to ask for it!

This book is designed as a fun, interactive way to understand and practice what consent is, what it isn't, how to ask for it, how to say no, and how to get help if someone doesn't respect your no.

Some of the topics can be scary (especially related to sexual abuse), so while it's important for your kids to have fun learning about consent, it's also important they understand consent is a life-changing, necessary skill used every day.

HI!, MY NAME IS KARL!.

Can I talk to you about
consent today?*

*If you say no, that's OK.
We'll try again another time!

Thanks for saying yes!

YOU JUST GAVE ME CONSENT!

Most people think consent is the same as giving someone permission.

But it's actually a lot more than that.

CONSENT IS A FRE

ELY GIVEN "YES."

"Freely given" means without any force.

Consent is something
you need to ask for,
or grant or deny,
every single time.

For example,

when my son, Ollie,
is sad or overwhelmed,
he often asks me for a hug.

But other times when he's upset,
he wants to be left alone.

Consent can look different every day,
and it can be different for every person.

Just because Ollie and I consent to hug or give kisses doesn't mean his grandma gets to kiss him whenever she wants.

She has to ask him first!

Because...

Consent is a 2-way conversation that always starts with a question.

Some of those questions sound like:

"CAN I BORROW YOUR PEN?"

"CAN I PET YOUR DOG OR CAT?"

"CAN I HAVE A HUG?"

"CAN I PLAY WITH YOU?"

"CAN I HAVE A BITE OF YOUR FOOD?"

Sometimes the answer will be yes.

Sometimes the answer will be no.

Sometimes the answer will be:

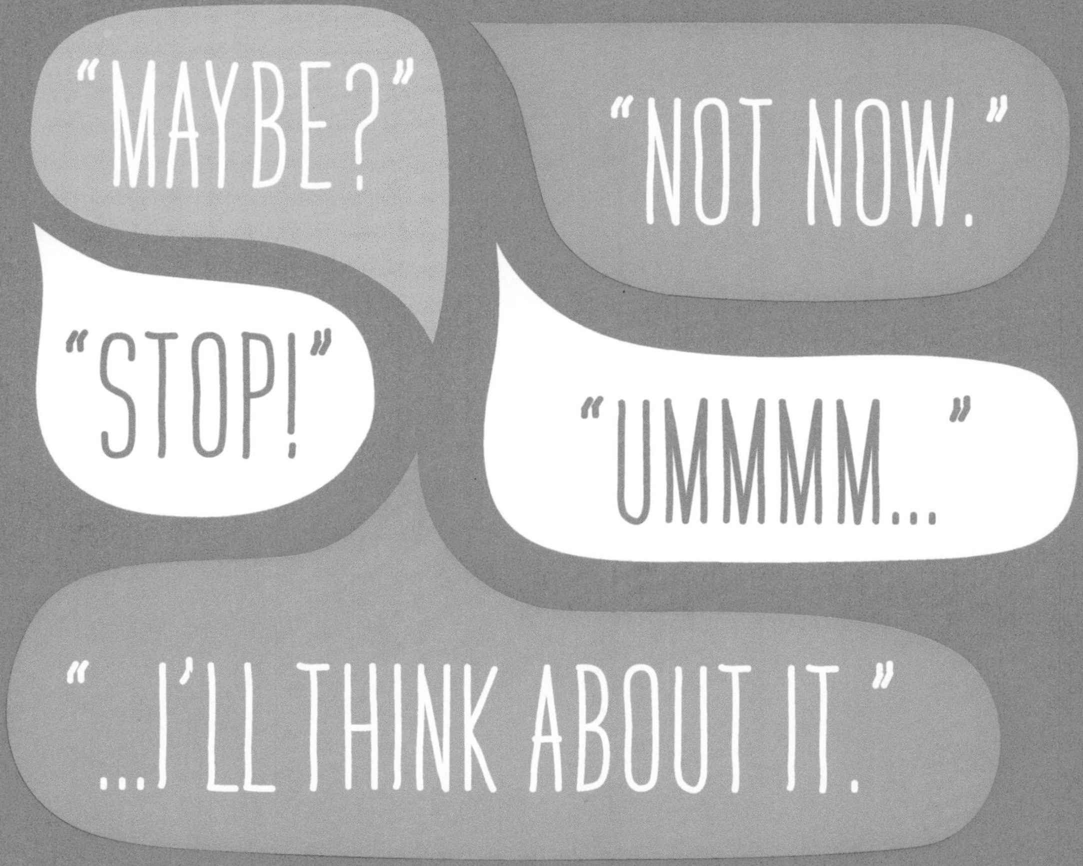
"MAYBE?"
"NOT NOW."
"STOP!"
"UMMMM..."
"...I'LL THINK ABOUT IT."

Those are also ways to say no.

Sometimes the answer will start with a yes and change to a no.

And sometimes the answer will be yes, but they may not mean it.

So, how can we tell when someone doesn't really want to say yes?

Start by checking their body language and tone of voice!

DID THEY LOOK DOWN?

HOW DID THEY SAY "YES" OR "NO"?

DID THEY FROWN?

WAS THEIR VOICE QUIET?

WERE THEIR ARMS CROSSED?

If someone's body looks like this when you ask for consent, the answer is always no.

IT, WAIT...

I know it might sound confusing that people may say yes when they actually don't want to.

But sometimes people only say yes because they feel like they have to.

When someone really wants to say yes, they may smile, sound happy or excited, approach you, and give a confident...

"YES."

Consent should always
be enthusiastic!

So, we understand that

"no" means "no"

and that

"yes" doesn't always mean "yes."

When someone says no,
or they look scared, confused,
or aren't able to say no,
that doesn't mean you keep
pushing until you get a "yes."

Remember, consent is something that is freely given.

When that's not the case, it's not consent.

Consent means saying yes because you want to, and not because you're forced to.

Now, that isn't the same thing as when grownups who care for us tell us to do things that are good for our health, but aren't always what we want to do.

"GET IN THE BATHTUB!"

"WEAR A COAT!"

"EAT YOUR VEGGIES!"   "STOP RUNNING!"

This is different from when someone forces you to do something that makes you feel unsafe!

Some of those unsafe forces look like...

GUILT:

Someone makes you feel sad for not saying yes the first time.

Example: "Grandpa says you hurt their feelings because you won't hug them."

PEER PRESSURE:

Being negatively influenced by kids your own age.

Example: "You're not cool if you don't go to the scary movie with us!"

PHYSICAL:

Someone touches, hits, or hurts you.

Example: You say no to a hug, but a grownup picks you up and gives you a big hug anyway.

DRUGS AND/OR ALCOHOL:

Someone gives you a substance to make your body do something it doesn't want to.

Example: You're given a drug which makes you so tired you fall asleep. You can't say no to things you don't want when you're sleeping.

THREAT:

Someone says they'll do something bad in response to your actions.

Example: "If you don't hug me, I'll hurt your dog."

BLACKMAIL:

Someone knows you did something you aren't proud of, and they threaten to tell if you don't do what they want.

Example: You sneak an extra cookie and your big cousin says to you, "I'll tell on you if you don't do what I say."

MISUSE OF TRUST:

A grownup in charge, who you trust, does something you're uncomfortable with.

Example: Your teacher asks you to stay after school to talk when you don't want to be left alone with them.

I know all of this sounds scary.

It was really scary when
it happened to me.

One of my close friends used some of these forces to get me to do something I didn't want to do.

But I didn't give a strong "no" because I was too shocked and scared.

It will never be OK what happened to me, but it's OK if it feels too difficult to speak up in the moment.

If you find yourself in a similar situation, you can try walking away, saying you have to use the bathroom, or telling the person you feel sick.

And remember: If someone tells *you* these things, they want to be left alone.

If something happens to you that you didn't consent to, as soon as you are able to, tell a grownup you trust.

At first, I was embarrassed. I didn't totally understand what happened, but I knew it was wrong.

Eventually, I found the courage to tell someone, and I got the help I needed.

AND LOOK A

I wrote this book because it's important for

T ME NOW!

every kid and grownup to know consent.

So, let's practice what
we've learned today!

First, practice asking for
consent (because it always
starts with a question).

Turn to the person you're reading with and ask them for a high five.

How did they respond?

Did they shake their head or move their hand away?

Did they say no?

Or were they happy?

Did they raise their hand, excited to give you a high five?

SEE? CONSENT I

S SO MUCH FUN!

Now, let's practice saying no when someone asks you a question.

Turn to the person you're reading with and practice saying no when they ask you for a high five.

How did that feel for you?

Did they look sad when you said no?

Sometimes saying no is hard because other people might get their feelings hurt.

But your "no" is still important and how you feel matters.

When everyone asks for consent, and respects the given answer, the world is a safer and better place.

So, will you help me show the world what consent means?

Let me hear your biggest,
most enthusiastic,

YES!

(and it's OK if you choose to say no!)

Outro

See? Consent is fun! Now that you have a better understanding of consent and have practiced, don't stop! Consent is a continual conversation and skill that should be used daily.

Discuss your family's physical boundaries: "Do you like when I hug you when you come home from school? Or should I ask every time?"

Point out consent in television, movies, and books: "Should the prince kiss her if she's sleeping? Can you give consent if you're sleeping?"

Talk about boundaries with other friends and family: "Grandma is going to try to hug you. Let's practice saying no to her and coming to me for help if she doesn't listen."

The more your kid practices asking for consent and saying no, the more skills and confidence they will gain to prevent an unwanted situation!

If you or a loved one ever requires support in matters concerning sexual violence or abuse, please, contact the National Sexual Assault Hotline by calling 800.656.HOPE (4673) or chatting at hotline.rainn.org where you can receive 24/7 support.

About The Author

Karli Johnson M.S.Ed. (she/they) is a queer, disabled international TEDx speaker, educator, victim advocate, mental health activist, abuse survivor, and probably the world's best party starter.

As seen in her TEDx Talk, Karli uses humor, storytelling, and fun to discuss hard topics such as abuse, harassment, trauma, mental illness, and difficult communication.

Proud single mom, costume performer, former crisis advocate, and host of the "Ask For It" podcast, Karli worked with Illinois Representative Ann M. Williams on the 2019 consent education bill, requiring consent to be taught in Illinois schools' sex education. Karli speaks to schools, organizations, and businesses all over the world and is also a member of the RAINN Speakers Bureau.

Her mission is simple: prevent the bad, empower the good.

 @ mskarlijohnson   www.karlijohnson.com

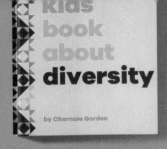

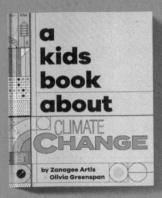

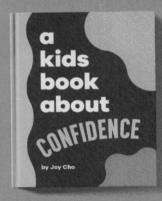

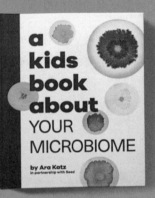
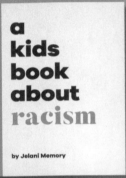

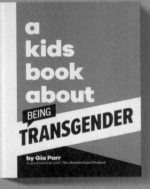